Voodoo Zombies

by Ruth Owen

Consultant: Luke W. Boyd
Editor in Chief
Zombie Research Society
Los Angeles, California

BEARPORT
PUBLISHING

New York, New York

Credits

Cover, © Yellowj/Shutterstock, © Andreas Gradin/Alamy, © Anneka/Shutterstock, © Jacob Lund/Shutterstock, © Annotee/Shutterstock, and © Stepan Kapl/Shutterstock; 3L, © froe_mic/Shutterstock; 4–5, © Kim Jones; 6, © LoveVectorGirl/Shutterstock and © Nomad_Soul/Shutterstock; 7T, © Dawn J Benko/Shutterstock; 7B, © Robert Estall Photo Agency/Alamy; 8, © weera sreesan/Shutterstock, © pathdoc/Shutterstock, © mimagephotography/Shutterstock, and © Everett Historical/Shutterstock; 9, © Jean-Claude Francolon/Getty Images; 10L, © Hector Retamal/Getty Images; 10R, © narvikk/Istock Photo; 11T, © Dieu Nalio Chery/A P Images; 11R, © Roman Cagnoni/Getty Images; 12, © Everett Historical/Shutterstock; 13, © Roger Hutchings/Alamy; 14–15, © Kim Jones; 14B, © Chronicle/Alamy; 16–17, © John North/Istock Photo; 17, © Renphoto/Istock Photo; 18L, © p_saranya/Shutterstock; 18R, © Wade Davis; 19TL, © Baimieng/Shutterstock; 19C, © BOONROONG/Shutterstock; 19R, © Steve Bower/Shutterstock; 19B, © antpkr/Shutterstock; 20L, © Warawanai Neko/Shutterstock; 20R, © Vastram/Shutterstock; 21, © diane39/Istock Photo; 22, © iJeab/Shutterstock, © Boltenkoff/Shutterstock, © windu/Shutterstock, and © Jag_cz/Shutterstock; 23, © Callahan/Shutterstock.

Publisher: Kenn Goin
Senior Editor: Joyce Tavolacci
Creative Director: Spencer Brinker
Photo Researcher: Ruth Owen Books

Library of Congress Cataloging-in-Publication Data

Names: Owen, Ruth, 1967– author.
Title: Voodoo zombies / by Ruth Owen.
Description: New York : Bearport Publishing Company, Inc., 2018. I Series:
   Zombie zone I Includes bibliographical references and index.
Identifiers: LCCN 2017049028 (print) I LCCN 2017051077 (ebook) I
ISBN 9781684024971 (Ebook) I ISBN 9781684024391 (library)
Subjects: LCSH: Narcisse, Clairvius—Juvenile literature. I
   Vodou—Haiti—Biography—Juvenile literature. I Zombies—Juvenile
   literature.
Classification: LCC BL2490 (ebook) I LCC BL2490 .O94 2018 (print) I DDC
   299.6/75097294—dc23
LC record available at https://lccn.loc.gov/2017049028

For more information, write to Bearport Publishing Company, Inc., 45 West 21st Street, Suite 3B, New York, New York 10010. Printed in the United States of America.

10 9 8 7 6 5 4 3 2 1

Contents

Back from the Dead

It was a normal day in the village of L'Estere on the island of Haiti. As Angelina Narcisse strolled in the village market, she noticed a strange-looking man staring at her. Eventually, he staggered over to her. The man said he was Clairvius, her brother. Shocked and terrified, Angelina started to scream. Why was Angelina so upset? Her brother had been dead for nearly 20 years!

Eighteen years earlier on April 30, 1962, Clairvius Narcisse went to the hospital. He was burning with fever and coughing up blood. Soon, he was struggling to breathe. On May 2, doctors **pronounced** him dead. The next day, Clairvius was buried in the village cemetery.

Could it be possible that Clairvius Narcisse had returned from the dead . . . as a zombie?

The man who said he was Clairvius Narcisse was able to prove his **identity** by telling Angelina his childhood nickname. Only his family members had known that name.

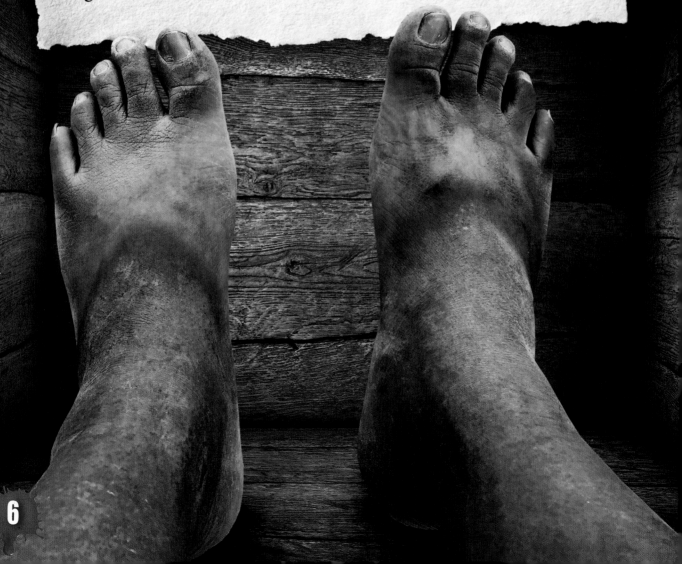

Buried Alive!

Once he was reunited with his sister, Clairvius had an unbelievable and **nightmarish** tale to tell. He told Angelina that in May 1962, when the doctors pronounced him dead, he could still hear and feel. For example, he heard Angelina weeping at his bedside. He also felt the doctors pull a sheet over his body. Then, unable to move or speak, Clairvius remembers being taken to the graveyard in a wood **coffin**—and buried alive!

Clairvius did not know how long he lay in the cold ground. Then he felt his coffin being cracked open. A gang of men, led by a **sorcerer** called a **bokor**, pulled him from his grave. Clairvius was tied up and taken to a sugar **plantation**, where he was forced to work.

Clairvius felt as if he was in a **trance** and could not think for himself. He realized the bokor had turned him into a zombie slave!

As the lid of his coffin was nailed shut, Clairvius felt one of the nails pierce his skin. He had a scar on his face from the wound.

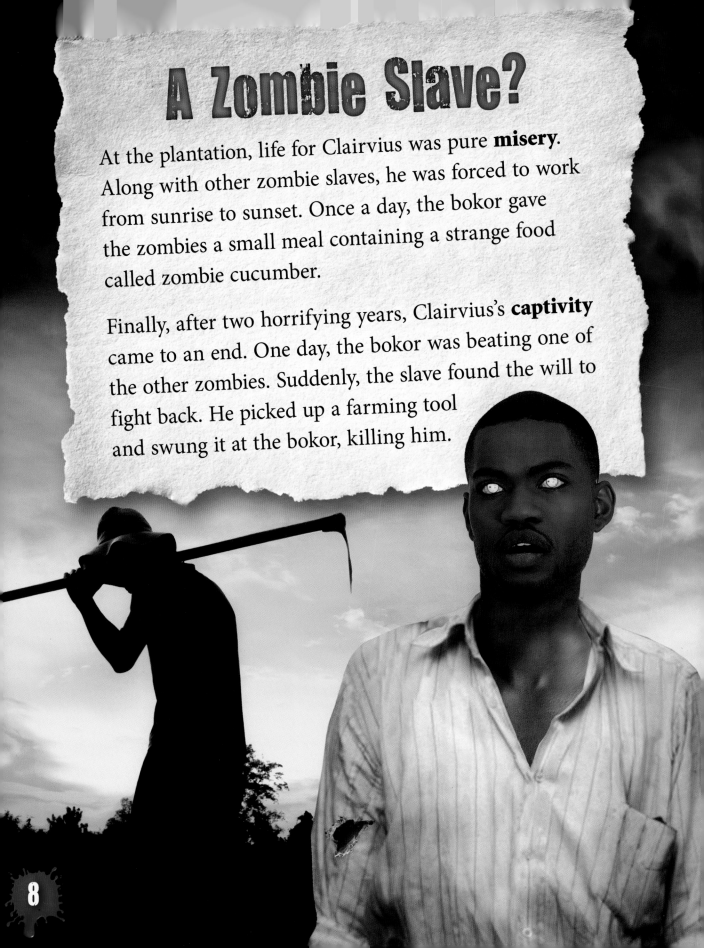

A Zombie Slave?

At the plantation, life for Clairvius was pure **misery**. Along with other zombie slaves, he was forced to work from sunrise to sunset. Once a day, the bokor gave the zombies a small meal containing a strange food called zombie cucumber.

Finally, after two horrifying years, Clairvius's **captivity** came to an end. One day, the bokor was beating one of the other zombies. Suddenly, the slave found the will to fight back. He picked up a farming tool and swung it at the bokor, killing him.

Once the bokor was dead, Clairvius and the other zombies escaped. For the next 16 years, Clairvius lived in the countryside until he finally returned to his village. Was Clairvius's story true? Could an evil sorcerer turn a human into a zombie?

Clairvius Narcisse sitting on the tomb where he says he was buried

Clairvius believed his brother had paid the bokor to turn him into a zombie after a family disagreement. Only when his brother died did Clairvius finally return to his family.

Murder and Magic

On the island of Haiti, many people believe in zombies. This belief comes from a religion called **voodoo**. According to old tales, evil voodoo bokors use magic to create zombies. To do this, it's said a bokor first kills a victim by putting a highly poisonous powder on the person's skin. Once the victim is dead and buried, the bokor digs up the body. The bokor then uses magic to bring the **corpse** back from the dead. He feeds the zombie a special fruit known as a zombie cucumber to keep it in a trance-like state.

Voodoo is a religion from Africa. When people were taken from Africa and enslaved on Haiti, they brought their religion with them. Today, many Haitians still practice voodoo.

Making zombie powder

A voodoo believer at a sacred pool in Haiti

Why would an evil bokor create a zombie? Some Haitians believe that bokors turn their enemies into the walking dead. A victim might also be zombified in order to force him into slavery.

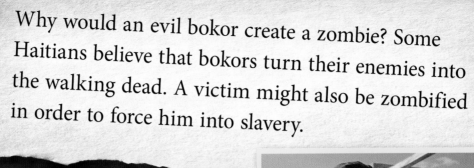
These Haitian men are dressed up like zombies for a voodoo ceremony.

A skull and other items used in voodoo rituals

A Fate Worse than Death

In Haiti, the belief in magic, witchcraft, and zombies is very powerful. For many Haitians, the fear of being a slave is all too real. Beginning in the 1500s, the **ancestors** of modern-day Haitians were forced into slavery. Millions of people were made to work without pay and treated **brutally**. In 1804, the Haitian people fought for and won their freedom. To a Haitian person, the thought of becoming a zombie slave is a fate worse than death.

Enslaved people at a sugarcane plantation in the 1500s

Toussaint L'Ouverture, the leader of Haitian independence

In recent times, to keep a bokor from zombifying dead bodies, some Haitians ask for their graves to be covered by huge rocks. Other people are laid to rest in large **tombs** sealed shut with a heavy lock. Despite these **precautions**, many terrible tales of zombies remain.

Large concrete tombs at a cemetery in Haiti

The word *zombie* may come from two different African languages. Some experts think it's formed from the words *ndzumbi*, which means "corpse," and *nzambi*, which means "spirit of a dead person."

From Zombies to Corpses

One horrifying story from 1918 tells of a bokor named Ti Joseph and his band of zombies. Joseph's zombie slaves worked on a sugarcane plantation. The mindless zombies were paid for their work, but their evil master, Joseph, took their money and kept it for himself.

According to the tale, one day when Joseph was away, his wife, feeling sorry for the zombies, took them to see a parade. She gave each zombie a small handful of candy to eat that contained salty peanuts.

An American explorer named William Seabrook visited Haiti in the early 1900s. Local people told him the **eerie** story of Ti Joseph's zombies. No one can say, however, if the story is true.

Amazingly, the salt broke the spell that controlled the zombies. The poor creatures began to howl as they realized they were walking corpses! They staggered back to their village and into the cemetery. There, they clawed and dug at their own graves with their bare hands. Then the zombies crawled back down into the cold earth. Their bodies immediately began to decay and turn to dust.

A Strange Visitor

Another famous zombie encounter took place in 1936 in the Haitian village of Emery. On the morning of October 24, an old woman in ragged clothes limped into the village. Her wrinkled skin looked like dry fish scales and all her eyelashes had fallen out. The woman could not speak and seemed to be in a trance.

As the villagers gathered to see the strange visitor, they were overcome with fear. They believed she was a corpse that had come back to life as a zombie!

To their horror, one local family felt sure they knew the woman. She was their relative Felicia Felix-Mentor, who had died 30 years before!

Was the strange visitor Felicia Felix-Mentor? When she was taken to a hospital, doctors discovered the truth. The woman was very ill, which explained why she looked and behaved the way she did. Also, she was not Felicia Felix-Mentor—and she was definitely not a zombie.

Searching for the Truth

If the mysterious stories of voodoo zombies are true, is it because bokors have magical powers? Or can science offer an explanation?

In the early 1980s, a young Canadian scientist named Wade Davis went to Haiti to investigate the **phenomenon**. Davis visited bokors and obtained samples of their deadly zombie powders. He tested them and discovered they contained a poison called tetrodotoxin, which comes from the bodies of puffer fish.

Wade Davis

A fisherman holding a puffer fish

If this powerful poison enters a person's bloodstream, the victim's heartbeat slows down. The person might almost stop breathing and fall into a deep **coma**. In fact, a person who was poisoned by tetrodotoxin could seem dead—even to a doctor. Once the effects of the poison wear off, however, the person might wake up. Then it would appear as if a corpse had come back to life!

Davis's tests showed that zombie powder can also contain bits of toads, tree frogs, lizards, and centipedes. Some powders also contained human bones that had been burned and crushed.

Science or Magic?

Wade Davis had a theory. He believed that bokors poisoned their victims with puffer fish. If the victim survived and woke up, the bokor would claim it was due to magic. A survivor might be brain damaged and sick, which could make the person appear to be a zombie.

To control the zombielike person, a bokor might then feed the victim a paste made of zombie cucumber. This poisonous fruit comes from the highly toxic datura plant. A person who regularly eats datura might become dazed, confused, and suffer from memory loss.

In zombie folklore, it's said that a zombie must not eat salt or the bokor's spell will be broken. Humans need salt or else they will feel very weak. So, do bokors make their victims weary and zombielike by keeping them from eating salt?

The flowers of a datura plant

Datura fruit, or zombie cucumber

So, what is the truth? Some scientists agree with Davis's theory that poison is used to create zombielike humans. Other scientists strongly disagree.

Will the mystery of voodoo zombies one day be solved by science? Or is there a more terrifying truth yet to be discovered?

Get Creative, Writers!

Use the stories in this book to help get your creative zombie juices flowing! Write two or three questions or sentences for each writing prompt below.

Zombie Reporter

Imagine you are a news reporter. You have been sent to interview Clairvius Narcisse after his return from the dead.

- What three questions would you like to ask him?
- Can you think of additional questions to test if his story is actually true?

Cemetery Witness

Imagine you are visiting an old Haitian cemetery at night. You witness a voodoo bokor raising a corpse from its grave!

- What does the bokor do and say?
- How does the zombie look and act?

My Life as a Voodoo Zombie!

What would it be like to be turned into a voodoo zombie? Imagine this terrible fate has befallen you.

- How did it feel when the bokor raised you from the dead?
- What's it like not to be able to talk or ask for help?

Remember to use descriptive details!

Glossary

ancestors (AN-sess-turz) family members who lived a long time ago

bokor (BOH-kur) a voodoo sorcerer who is believed to use magic for evil purposes

brutally (BROO-tuh-lee) in a savage or violent way

captivity (kap-TIV-uh-tee) the state of being held in a place where one cannot escape

coffin (KAWF-in) a long box in which a dead person is buried

coma (KOH-muh) a state in which a person cannot wake up

corpse (KORPS) a dead body

eerie (EER-ee) weird and scary

identity (eye-DEN-ti-tee) who someone is

misery (MIH-zuh-ree) great unhappiness

nightmarish (NITE-mair-ish) horrible or terrifying, as if from a nightmare

phenomenon (fi-NOM-uh-non) something that is extraordinary and hard to explain

plantation (plan-TAY-shuhn) a large farm where crops are grown

precautions (pri-KAW-shuhnz) actions taken to keep something from happening

pronounced (pruh-NOUNST) announced in an important and definite way

sorcerer (SOR-sur-er) a person who performs magic

tombs (TOOMZ) places where people are buried

trance (TRANSS) a state between sleeping and waking in which a person may not be able to think

voodoo (VOO-doo) a religion that includes some traditional African beliefs

Index

Read More

Bailey, Diane. *Zombies in America (America's Supernatural Secrets).* New York: Rosen (2012).

Kamberg, Mary-Lane. *Investigating Zombies and the Living Dead (Understanding the Paranormal).* New York: Rosen (2015).

Owen, Ruth. *Becoming a Zombie (Zombie Zone).* New York: Bearport (2018).

Learn More Online

To learn more about voodoo zombies, visit
www.bearportpublishing.com/ZombieZone

About the Author

Ruth Owen has been developing and writing children's books for more than 10 years. She lives in Cornwall, England, just minutes from the ocean. If there's a zombie apocalypse, she intends to escape by boat!